98

j636   Wexler, Jerome.
WEX
        Pet mice

$13.95

DATE			

PET MICE

Text and photos by JEROME WEXLER

Albert Whitman & Company, Niles, Illinois

Library of Congress Cataloging-in-Publication Data

Wexler, Jerome.
    Pet mice.

    Summary: Text and color photographs describe how to
house, feed, and handle a pair of pet mice and the
families they produce.
    1. Mice as pets—Juvenile literature. [1. Mice
as pets] I. Title.
SF459.M5W49   1989   636'.93233   88-2
ISBN 0-8075-6524-5

Table of Contents

Ooh—how cute! Can I touch one? Can I pick one up? Can I take one home? Can I take *all* of them home?

A pet mouse will run up your arm and poke in your pocket for a treat. It's fun to watch a mouse eat and play, or maybe you would enjoy taking photos of it or keeping a diary of its life. If you have a male and a female, the two will play, eat, and sleep together and then one morning—surprise! In a corner of the cage, you'll find a nest of pink babies.

Before you begin
Keeping mice is easy. They don't take up much room, and there aren't many hard-and-fast rules for taking care of them. All it takes is a little knowledge and some common sense. But you can't just buy a couple of mice and bring them home. You need to do some thinking and make some plans.

Where will you keep your mice? What will you feed them? How will you catch them if they get away? What will you do if they have babies? How will you feel six months from now after having cleaned their cage over fifty times? (The job has to be done at least twice a week if you have a male.) Don't forget your family—how will everyone feel about having mice in the house? The more problems you solve before buying your mice, the happier you, your family, and your mice will be.

About mice

Scientists organize all living things into groups. Mice belong to a class, or group, called mammals. All mammals are warm-blooded, have hair on their bodies, and feed their young milk. You and I and all human beings are also mammals.

Rodents are one of the many kinds of mammals. Mice, rats, squirrels, beavers, porcupines, woodchucks, prairie dogs, chipmunks, and rabbits are all rodents. Rodents have very sharp front teeth called *incisors*, which grow continuously throughout their lives. They also have back teeth, or *molars*,

which they use for chewing. But there are no teeth between the incisors and molars—only a large space. Rodents mature quickly and have many offspring. A one-month-old mouse can become pregnant and three weeks later give birth to as many as twelve babies.

In the wild, an animal is sometimes born with hair of an unusual color. Such an animal stands out, and it is usually seen and killed by a predator before it has a chance to breed and pass the new color on to its children. But an animal in captivity can be bred so that a new color is saved and passed on from generation to generation. This is what has happened to pet mice. Wild field mice are mostly gray, but pet mice are available in many colors: white, black, cream, blue, red, chocolate, dove, silver, tan, pink, and mixtures of two or more of these shades.

While not as tame and friendly as cats or dogs, pet mice have been bred to be more gentle than wild mice and can be trained to do simple tricks.

A mouse house

Where will you keep your mice? A standard ten-gallon glass aquarium makes a perfect home for a small group or a family. An aquarium is inexpensive and easy to clean. Litter won't fall out of it. Best of all, the mice can be seen from every side.

The exact number of mice that can be kept in any container depends on how easygoing the group is. A ten-gallon aquarium can usually accommodate an adult male or six adult females or a mother and father with a family of ten or twelve youngsters. Never put two adult males in the same cage; they will only fight.

Because mice like to jump and climb, you will need to buy a standard wire-mesh aquarium cover to put on top. The wire mesh will allow fresh air to circulate. It will also keep other animals from getting into the cage and harming your mice.

Mice can live in a wire cage, but it's not as much fun to watch them through the bars, and unless the bars are closely spaced, the babies can fall through! A wooden cage is not a good idea because urine will soak into the wood, causing a permanent odor. Worse, the mice can eat through the wood and escape. Litter from a wire or wooden cage will quickly scatter onto the floor.

No matter where your mice live, you will need to move them to a temporary home when you clean the cage or if a mouse gets sick. A small aquarium, a metal or plastic pail, a wastebasket, or almost any container at least twelve inches high with slippery sides will hold mice for a short time.

A bedroom, den, or family room is an excellent place to keep the cage. Like humans, mice prefer a temperature between sixty-five and eighty-five degrees F. If you feel comfortable, your mice will feel comfortable. Keep the cage out of damp, drafty areas and direct sunlight. If your house is very hot in the summer, you can move the cage to the coolest part of the room, which is usually near the floor.

Bedding

To absorb urine and any water that may spill, you will need to put bedding on the bottom of the cage. The bedding should be light and fluffy and free of dust. Pet stores sell several kinds, including wood chips, wood shavings, dried, crushed corncobs, and dried alfalfa or timothy hay. You can also make your own bedding from dried grass clippings (if the grass is free of pesticides) or shredded paper (if the paper has no printing on it).

All kinds of bedding are shown in the photos in this book. The bedding *I* like best is the dried, crushed corncobs. The bedding my *mice* like best is the dried grass clippings. They love to make tunnels in the grass and then play follow the leader. And whenever they are hungry, the clippings provide them with a snack. The problem with grass bedding is that it does a poor job of absorbing liquids and has to be changed every few days.

Mice like to sleep in a bed or nest which they make out of whatever soft material is on hand. In addition to bedding, you should provide them with some unscented tissue (the perfume from scented tissue may make them sick), small pieces of cloth, or packaged nesting material. You will enjoy seeing how they shred the tissue or cloth to make their bed!

Cleaning the cage

Droppings, urine, and food will soon get into the bedding. (Mice are usually particular about where they urinate, but they defecate anywhere in the cage, even in the seed dish!) You will need to change the bedding and clean the cage every week if you have females but two or more times a week if you have a male. If the air in the cage smells bad, it's time for a cleaning.

Remove the mice and put them in a temporary home. Discard the old bedding, keeping only a small piece of the nest so the mice will have something that smells familiar when they move back in. If your cage is a glass aquarium, wash the floor and sides with warm, soapy water, then rinse and dry everything well. Cleaning a wooden cage is more difficult. It should be soaked in a solution of one part bleach to twenty parts soapy water, then rinsed well with clear water.

Wash and dry the food dish, waterer, toys, and anything else the mice have used. Only after the cage is completely dry (a wooden cage may take several days to dry) should you put in new bedding, food, water, toys, nesting material, and finally, your mice.

Water

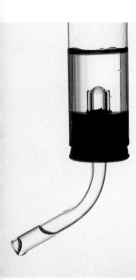

Mice drink a lot of water. A water dish can be set on the cage floor, but it will either quickly fill with litter and droppings or it will spill. It's better to use a gravity-feed waterer.

Pet stores stock several kinds. A type I *can't* recommend has a glass tube with an inside diameter of one-fourth inch. Because the tube is so small, there is a tendency for air pockets to form in it, as shown in the photo on the left. When this happens, the water can't flow through, and the mice can't drink. You can prevent this problem by using a container fitted with a stainless-steel tube that has a large diameter. To keep the water from running right out through the wider tube, a ball rests at the drinking end. When a mouse wants a drink, it pushes the ball up with its tongue or nose, and a drop of water comes out. Both the mouse and the cage stay dry. These waterers come in various sizes. The smallest can hold a two-or-three-weeks' supply of water for two mice, but you should replace the water twice a week. Hang the waterer so that the drinking tip is three to five inches from the bedding.

Cheese, please?

What do mice eat? Cheese? Well, a small amount once in a while may not do any harm. But wild mice normally eat seeds, plants, and insects, and pet mice should be given the same kinds of foods.

Mice should be fed a variety of seed. Mixes put together for finches or parakeets or sold as "wild birdseed" are fine. Just be sure the mix doesn't contain a lot of sunflower seeds. Mice love sunflower seeds, but they are rich in oils, and your pets don't need the extra calories. Some pet stores sell their own seed mixes. These are usually quite good and less expensive than brand-name seed.

Mice also like fruits and vegetables such as lettuce, dandelion leaves, carrots, cabbage, apples, and potatoes. They don't need much, though. Feed each

mouse only one piece of fruit or vegetable a day—a piece that weighs no more than a penny. Whatever isn't eaten within ten or fifteen minutes should be removed, as fresh food can quickly become moldy and may make your mice sick.

A vegetable food that can be left in the cage for a long time is dried alfalfa. The alfalfa can be purchased from a pet store in a loose or compressed form. Just place a small amount on the bedding. The mice will nibble on it whenever they are hungry, and what isn't eaten will be discarded when you change the bedding. I like to feed my mice fresh foods when I'm home and give them alfalfa when I go away for several days.

In the wild, mice eat insects for protein. For pet mice, dog biscuits are a good substitute. Mice really enjoy dog biscuits, and chewing on them is good for their teeth.

Some breeders advise giving mice a small amount of raw, lean meat once a week. Others say that feeding meat to mice encourages cannibalism—that is, the mice will eat each other or parent mice will eat their newborn babies. It's hard to know how your mice will react. Perhaps the safest course is to stick to a diet of seed, fruits, vegetables, and dog biscuits. These foods will provide all the protein and other nutrients your mice need.

Pet stores also sell pelleted feed. This is a scientific mix of ground seed, dried meats, bone meal, alfalfa, dried milk, vitamins, and minerals squeezed together to form small pellets for small animals and larger pellets for larger animals. Pelleted feed is nutritionally ideal, but if given a choice most mice prefer a variety of food. Buy a small amount first to see how your mice react.

All breeders agree on one thing: don't feed your mice human snack foods! Candy, potato chips, cake, cookies, and other sweet or oily foods will make the mice gain weight, spoil their appetite for good food, and may even make them sick.

To keep litter out of the food, you will need a deep dish. A ceramic or metal dish works very well, or if you don't mind it being slowly chewed away, you can use a plastic container such as a margarine tub. If you find that the mice still get litter in their food, try raising the dish an inch or two by nailing or gluing it to a small block of wood.

Because mice burn up energy quickly, they need to eat often. Be sure some food is always in the cage. If you place enough seed in the dish so that a small amount is left each day, you will know your mice are not hungry. (My mice consume about a level teaspoonful per mouse per day.) You don't need to worry that the mice will overeat; they will only take what they need and leave the rest. Each day, discard the old seed, wash and dry the dish, and refill it.

If your family goes away for a few days, put a lot of extra dry food—food pellets or seed, dog biscuits, and dried alfalfa—in the cage and make sure the waterer is full. Add an extra waterer if you have a family of mice. If you are going to be away longer than two weeks, ask a friend to take care of the mice.

Mouse toys

Your mice will be happier and healthier if they have plenty of exercise and some "toys" to play with. To provide them with enough exercise, buy them an exercise wheel. They will love it. Other good mouse toys can be found around the house. My mice like the tubes from paper towels or unscented toilet tissue. They run in and out of the tubes for hours and sometimes sleep in them. They also like climbing in and out of empty tissue boxes, and they spend hours chewing on small sticks. If you can't find a clean stick, try a wooden clothespin.

Fleas?

A mouse normally keeps its body clean. It spends a great deal of time washing itself (even its tail!) with its tongue and combing itself with its nails. Baby mice clean and comb themselves even before their eyes are open. Mice don't normally have fleas, lice, ticks, or other parasites. But you don't know if the mice you are going to buy were brought up under sanitary conditions. As a precaution, before buying your mice you should purchase a spray can of flea powder that is made for mice, gerbils, hamsters, or even cats. *Never* use dog insecticides—these are far too strong for mice. You will only have to spray a few times, so buy a small can.

The instructions will probably say to spray the animals, but I don't like doing this for fear of getting insecticide in their eyes. Instead, I lightly spray the floor of the cage. If this is done once a week for three or four weeks, all insect pests will be killed. As long as your mice are kept from other animals, there will be no need to use the insecticide again.

Getting the cage ready

Wash the cage, waterer, seed dish, and exercise wheel using a soft sponge and lots of soap and water. A ten-gallon aquarium is heavy, so you may need help with it. If the cage or any other item has ever been used by another animal, add bleach, such as Chlorox, to the wash water. Rinse everything well. When the cage is thoroughly dry, spray the insecticide into the four corners and one or two spots in the center of the floor. (Always wash your hands thoroughly with soap and water after using any kind of insecticide.) Let the floor dry, then cover it with about an inch of bedding. Put seed in the seed dish, fill the waterer (check to see that water is coming through), and set these and the exercise wheel in place. Put two or three pieces of cloth or tissue in one corner so the mice can make their bed.

Just in case . . .

All animals, wild or pet, sometimes bite. Before buying my mice, I visited my doctor and got a tetanus booster shot. If you've had one recently, you're all set. If not, check with your parents—they might want you to get one.

Buying the best mice

Ready? Let's go to the pet store!

You should visit several before buying your mice. Prices may vary, but what's most important is to find a store that is clean and takes good care of its animals. You should always buy pets that have been given lots of tender, loving care, even if they cost more.

Keep in mind that mice like the company of other mice. One mouse all by itself soon becomes listless and sleeps most of the time. To be happy and healthy, a single mouse needs a lot of attention from its owner, probably more attention than you can give it.

If you don't want to start a mouse family, it's best to buy two females because males will fight. Males also cause more odor problems than females because they spray urine to indicate their territory. If you have a male mouse, you may want to clean the cage as often as every day.

Look for young mice. The life span of a mouse is only two to three years, and you want to enjoy your mice as long as possible. Choose animals that are slender, lively, and alert. Their eyes should be wide open, clean, and bright—not closed or crusty. The fur should be glossy and thick, with no bald spots. Watch to see that the mice move around the cage quickly and smoothly. Don't buy a mouse that wheezes or coughs. Check the area under the base of the tail. If it's wet, the mouse probably has diarrhea, which can be caused by disease.

To take the pictures for this book, I set up two cages and bought two pairs

of mice. The first pair was a black-and-white male and a buff-and-white female. The second pair was just the opposite—a black-and-white female and a buff-and-white male. The pet store put the pairs in small cardboard containers—containers meant for birds. Mice like to chew, and by the time I got home, one had chewed a hole in the side of the box almost big enough to crawl through. Ask the pet store if they will double-box your mice or put the carton into a large paper bag. On the way home, keep an eye on the package!

When the mice come home

Put the mice in their cage right away. Remember, they are frightened and nervous. If you put your hand into the container to remove them, chances are you'll be bitten. Instead, place the box in the cage and open one end. Once the mice are out, they will scoot around their new home, sniffing here and there. Within minutes they will settle down enough to start eating. Enjoy watching them, but don't try to make friends yet. Don't even touch them. They've been through enough for one day. You might want to use this time to think of just the right names for your new pets.

Studying your mice

When the mice are relaxed, you can take a good look at them. A mature mouse is about three and a half to four inches long (males are a bit larger than females) and has a tail about as long as its body. Because of its thick coat of fur it looks heavy, but it weighs about the same as a small candy bar. My two males averaged 37 grams, and the females averaged 33 grams (28.3 grams = one ounce).

Although a mouse has large, bright eyes (with no noticeable eyelashes), it is nearsighted. It makes up for its poor sight with a strong sense of smell and keen hearing. With its sensitive white whiskers, which from tip to tip are almost as long as its body, a mouse can feel objects and find its way through narrow passageways, even at night.

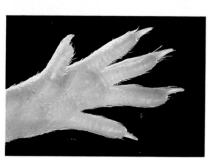

A mouse has five toes on its rear feet but only four on its front feet. The fifth toe, the thumb, is only a short stub.

Although a mouse has sixteen teeth (twelve molars and four incisors), we can see only the four front teeth, the incisors. There are two on the top and two on the bottom. Each set is sort of fused together so that at a quick glance, it appears to be a single tooth.

Like the incisor teeth of all rodents, the incisors of mice

grow continuously. A rodent must chew on hard substances to keep these teeth worn down, or they will grow so long they will interfere with the animal's ability to eat. It is very important to supply mice with hard things to chew on—small pieces of clean wood (no plywood or wood that has been painted), nuts in their shells, dog biscuits, pellets, and bones. Bones are especially good because they supply calcium.

Making friends

After the mice have been in their new home for a day or so, you can begin to make friends with them. It's not hard. But it takes time and patience, and you may suffer a bite or two. If you are bitten, simply wash the area with soap and water and have your mom or dad put an antiseptic on the wound.

This is how my mice and I got acquainted. On the first day, I started by talking softly to them. After a few minutes, I removed the cover of the cage, gently rested one hand on the bedding, and allowed the mice to come and sniff it. Then I went to the second cage. But this time when I put my hand on the bedding, one of the mice bit me and yes, it did hurt! After taking care of my wound, I put my hand back—this time moving more slowly. It took some time, but eventually both mice sniffed my hand without biting it.

On the second day, I again first talked to the animals for a few minutes. This time when I put my hand into the cages, I held a sunflower seed between my thumb and forefinger. It took a long time before one mouse worked up the courage to take the seed. I repeated this several times, allowing each mouse to remove seeds from my fingers.

On the third day, I talked to my mice and then placed several sunflower seeds in my palm, forcing them to step on my hand to retrieve the food.

On the fourth day, the female in one cage sat on my hand to eat, but the male attacked and bit me again. Several more days passed before all four mice would eat sitting on my hand. I must add that the males never really became friendly. And after babies were born, each became even more aggressive and very protective of their families.

Not everyone likes handling mice, but if you keep them as pets you will have to pick them up at least occasionally, to move them when their cage needs cleaning, to separate males from females, or to remove a sick mouse. If you've gotten a mouse to sit on your palm, you can simply cup your hand and slowly lift the mouse out of the cage. For more security, you can form a roof over the mouse with your other hand. It's also easy to transport a mouse in a container such as a large cup, a small flowerpot, or a clean tin can (be sure it has no sharp edges). Put seed in the container and, as soon as the mouse enters, cover the opening with your hand or a piece of cardboard. Now you can move the mouse wherever you like.

Another way to pick up a mouse is to grab its tail *near the base* and quickly lift and place the mouse on your other hand or into a container. *Never* grab the tip of a mouse's tail—you may pull off the skin.

If you are very uneasy about handling a mouse, you can put on leather gloves.

Mice easily become frightened, so no matter how you handle them, always remember to be very gentle.

Training

Some mice are easy to train, and some are hard. It's easier to train females than males and young mice than older ones. If you have problems with your older mice, you may have to wait until they have a family and then work with the babies.

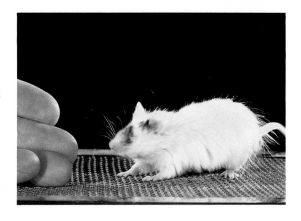

After your mice have learned to sit on your hand, you can try training them outside the cage. Begin with one mouse at a time. Put it on top of the aquarium (on the wire-mesh cover) or on a small table. The mouse will have room to move about, but since mice are afraid of heights, it won't jump off.

Because the mouse is in a new environment, it will be fearful and freeze in one spot for a few minutes. As it relaxes, it will begin to raise its body and look around. Give it a few more minutes by itself, and you will see it get up and begin to explore its new environment. When it looks relaxed, you can start training it.

When training your mouse, remember to move slowly. A sudden movement might frighten it so much that it will bite to protect itself or jump off your hand and run away.

You can teach a mouse to walk up your arm and sit on your shoulder, climb a ladder, jump through a hoop, or run through a maze. The secret is to coax it by offering a bit of food such as a sunflower seed. If you consistently place a seed in one pocket, for example, the mouse will soon learn to go directly to that pocket. Training a

mouse to sit up and beg like a dog is especially easy. Just hold some food above your mouse's nose—it will sit up to take the food from your fingers. Remember, each time the mouse does what you want, you must reward it with a treat.

The more you play with your mice, the tamer they will be. Three, four, or five times a day is not too often. Sometimes you might just hold them and stroke them—they will like that.

Remember, it's not a requirement that you train your mice. I've had many caged pets, and I have seldom trained any to do more than come to my hand for a goody. I just enjoy watching them as they live their lives in their cage, undisturbed by me.

There's a mouse loose!

What if a mouse gets loose? Immediately, close the door of the room. This will keep the mouse in a confined area and protect it from any other animal you may have. None of my mice have ever escaped, but I deliberately let one go to test a mousetrap called the Havahart Animal Trap. These traps capture an animal but do not harm it in any way. One evening, I set the trap on the floor in the center of the room, baited it with a piece of carrot, and then set its sensitive mechanism. After closing the door, I freed one mouse. In the morning there it was, caught and unharmed. The traps are not expensive, and if you are going to play with your mice outside their cage, you should buy one.

A cheaper but trickier way to catch an escaped mouse is to take some books and stack them to form a "stairway." Put some food in a wastebasket and lean

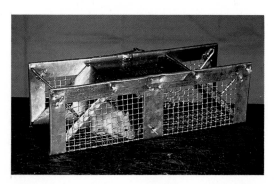

24

it against the topmost book. The mouse will smell the food, climb up the books, and slide down the wastebasket to get at it. If the angle of the wastebasket is sharp enough, the mouse won't be able to climb out.

A mouse family

If you spend a lot of time with your mice, you may one day see the male mounting the female. He will stay on her for only a few seconds, but he will mount her many times that day. Mark the date on your calendar, for some eighteen to twenty-two days later, chances are that the female will have babies.

If the female becomes pregnant, you will notice that she gets bigger and bigger around her middle. She eats more but continues to exercise as before.

Shortly before the mother gives birth, she goes through a stage called *labor*. She becomes nervous and loses interest in food, water, or exercise. She goes into a corner of the cage to be alone, or if you have provided a nesting box (you can buy one at a pet store), she goes inside the box. Leave the mother alone if you see her acting like this—

26

don't try to move her or even touch her. Many changes are occurring in her body to allow the babies to pass through what is usually a very small opening called the vagina. (The vagina in mice is normally about $\frac{1}{16}''$ in diameter, about the width of the lead in a pencil. When born, the babies are about $\frac{3}{8}''$ in diameter—six times larger than the normal size of the vagina.)

Each baby is born in a sac. As the sac containing the baby emerges from the mother's body, the mother grabs it, rips it open, and bites off the umbilical cord, releasing the baby. She then eats the sac. You may think eating the birth sac is disgusting, but most mammals do this to keep the nest clean.

During the birthing you may see a little blood. This is normal—you don't need to be concerned about it.

The mother washes and rubs each newborn baby with her tongue. This stimulation causes the baby to begin to breathe. Most baby mice are rather strong at birth. They crawl away from the mother even while being washed, so she has room in front of her for the next baby. The time between births can be as short as three minutes or as long as fifteen minutes. The delivery of a large litter of twelve or more mice may take several hours.

A baby mouse is called a *pup*, and together the pups are called a *litter*, just as with dogs. The mother is called a *doe* and the father a *buck*. A mouse litter can consist of just one pup or as many as fifteen. The average litter is five or six pups. Usually, the larger the litter, the smaller each pup.

After all the babies are born, the mother may rest, or she may get up and walk around or eat or even play on the exerciser. Every once in a while she may go over and look at her children, but it seems as if she doesn't know what to make of them. She may even nuzzle or pick one up and then drop it and walk away. Don't worry. This is normal. The babies are fine, and soon their mother will begin to take care of them.

Watching the birthing

Many authorities suggest that pregnant mice be provided with a closed nesting box and special nesting material. It is also advised that during birth and for about a week afterward, neither the mother nor the babies be touched. This is probably a good rule to follow to be sure the mother isn't upset in any way. But if you use a nesting box, you won't be able to see the babies being born.

If you want to watch the birthing, you must remove all of the bedding material (the shredded tissue and cloth) as soon as the mother goes into labor. Otherwise, she will make a nest and most of the delivery will be hidden from view. Mice often give birth at night, but all of mine have delivered sometime between 3:00 and 8:00 P.M. If your mice follow this pattern, it is quite possible to watch the event.

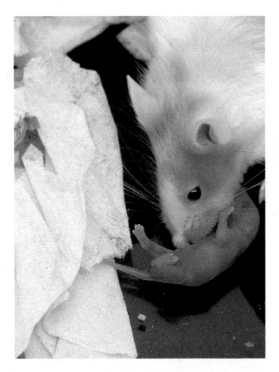
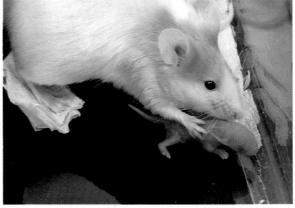

Some breeders advise taking the male out of the cage before the female goes into labor. I decided to leave the father in, though, as the mother and father are not separated in the wild. Once labor starts, the male and female move to opposite ends of the cage. The father stays away from the mother until the last baby is born, and then he very carefully and slowly moves toward her, as if watching for some signal that she is again ready for his companionship.

After the babies are born, you can provide the mother with a nesting box and nesting material, or you can give her some clean tissue. In either case, she will soon make a nest and move the babies to it. But, once again, if you give her a nesting box, the babies will be hidden from view. You won't see them again until they are old enough to crawl.

My mice have brought up many families without ever seeing a nesting box or using any special nesting material other than tissue. Mice are very adaptable, and they usually adjust to whatever conditions are available.

The birth photos
As a person who knows how to work with animals, I have been able to touch the mother during labor and birth. I have taken pups that were only two or three minutes old away from their mother, weighed and photographed them, and then returned them fifteen to twenty minutes later without any problems. *My experience* and *my mice* have allowed me to do this. Your experience and your mice may not. The best advice I can give is to look and not touch for at least two days. If you must touch the mother or babies, watch carefully to see how the mother reacts. If she shows signs of being agitated, stop!

Mice fathers

Female mice are able to become pregnant about every thirtieth day, give or take a day or two. Shortly after giving birth, the doe is ready to mate again. She can have another litter about twenty days later, even while nursing the first litter. If this is the only litter you want, *you must remove the buck as soon as the doe goes into labor and keep him out for forty-eight hours.* If the male is kept away for two days, the female will not become pregnant during this cycle. But in another thirty days or so she can become pregnant again, so when the pups are twenty-six or twenty-seven days old the buck must be taken out again. This time he must be removed forever, because he can mate with any of his female children as well as with their mother, and it is likely he will fight with his male children once they have become sexually mature.

If you plan to return the father to help raise the litter, be sure to do so after the pups are two days old but before they are three days old. If the buck and doe are separated for too long she may not accept him and may even attack him. If the father is returned soon enough, he is usually allowed to join the mother and babies in the nest, and for the next twenty-seven days the family will eat, sleep, and play together.

Mice fathers seem to be very good parents. They often babysit when the mother is away and are very protective of the pups. I have found it best not to try to remove a baby when the father is on guard.

A mouse diary

ONE DAY OLD: A newborn baby mouse is very small and weighs less than a penny! It appears pink but actually has hardly any color. Its skin is almost transparent, and the "pink" comes from the color of its flesh. The pup's eyes are closed, and its ears are very small and lie flat against its head. A newborn mouse has no noticeable hair on its body, but it does have short, transparent whiskers and short nails on front and back feet.

When the mother is in the nest, the pups crawl to her, find a nipple, and nurse. To let the pups get to the nipples, the mother often lifts her body and seems to stand on her toes. While the pups are small, the nest is very important, and both the mother and father help build and maintain it.

TWO DAYS OLD: Look at the pup in the center of the picture on page 35. It has just finished nursing, and its skin is still so thin and transparent you can see the milk in its stomach.

33

FIVE DAYS OLD: Below on the left is the pup's first formal portrait. Its hair is beginning to grow, and its ears have lifted off its head and are beginning to look mouselike.

SEVEN DAYS OLD: Their eyes are still closed, but the pups are very active—so active that each had to be placed in a container to be weighed. In one week the little mouse on the scale more than doubled its weight. The parents are very protective and will attack if someone gets too close.

ELEVEN DAYS OLD: The pups' weight is increasing fast—they now weigh up to three times as much as they did when born. The nest is continually being rebuilt by both parents.

THIRTEEN DAYS OLD: The whiskers and fur are developing nicely. The eyes of some of the pups are beginning to open, and the incisor teeth are emerging.

FIFTEEN DAYS OLD: Apparently the nest is becoming less important, for the parents don't spend much time rebuilding it. Some of the pups crawl away for short periods of time. As they explore, they find and eat bits of food.

This is a good time to begin handling the pups. Move slowly and touch them gently, and they will show very little fear.

It has been two weeks since the cage was cleaned. Now the pups can be handled, so this is a good time to do the job. Be careful moving the adults—

they may bite. Remember, they are trying to protect their babies. You might want to use a container to move them. When restocking the cage, fill the food dish for the parents and place a small amount of seed or pellets for the pups in one corner of the floor.

TWENTY-ONE DAYS OLD: The pups' eyes are now fully open, and their ears are almost full-grown. They no longer want to stay in the nest. The parents chase after them, grab them by the ears, and pull them back. But it's all in vain, and after a few hours the parents give up and the pups are free to roam. The pups' average weight is 11.7 grams, almost six times as much as they weighed at birth.

TWENTY-TWO TO TWENTY-EIGHT DAYS OLD: Life now changes fast for the pups. The youngsters explore everywhere and everything. They find the waterer and learn to drink from it. They still nurse, but they also eat seed and other bits of food. (This is the time to introduce them to new foods such as greens and fruits.) They locate the corner in which their parents urinate, and they start using that corner, too. They quickly learn to sit on their rumps and eat using their hands.

 The pups learn much by copying their parents and each other. If one starts to groom itself, they all groom themselves. If one goes to sleep, they all go to sleep.

Another mouse family?

Mice grow rapidly. A twenty-eight-day-old female can become pregnant; young males become sexually active about a week later. You must now ask yourself if you want to raise any more mice. I strongly advise against it.

Let's do a little math. It's possible for a female mouse to have as many as fifteen litters a year. The average litter contains six pups. That means that one female mouse could have ninety pups in only a year's time! How would you find homes for all these mice? Will your friends take some? (You'd better check with their parents first!) Will the pet store take some? (Don't guess—ask the manager.) If you cannot find good homes, you must separate all the males from the females before the pups are twenty-seven days old.

Female mice usually get along fine together, so all the females can go into one cage. (A ten-gallon aquarium can usually accommodate six females.) You can try putting males that have lived together in one cage, but you will need to check them several times each day. If you see signs of fighting, immediately separate the males, putting each into its own cage. If you see a fight, don't reach in with your bare hands! Push a piece of cardboard between the two fighting mice and then take one of them out.

Remember—never put two strange males in one cage. They will fight until one is killed. You may want to give some of the males away if they don't get along together and seem listless living separately.

Now comes the big question: how do you tell male from female mice? The key is the distance between the anus and the genitals. In a female, the distance is about one-fourth of an inch; in a male, about three-eighths of an inch.

Pick up two mice, one in each hand, and compare one against the other. Keep comparing mice until you are certain you are holding a male and a female. By studying these two for a few minutes, you will be able to sex the entire litter quickly and correctly.

Again, never pick a mouse up by the tip of the tail, for the skin may come off. The mouse will not squirm if you allow it to rest its forelegs on your other hand or if you give it a small piece of tissue to hold onto. The mouse is not in pain, so you don't need to rush.

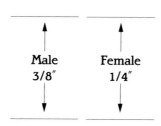

Male
3/8″

Female
1/4″

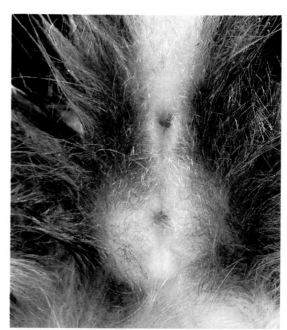

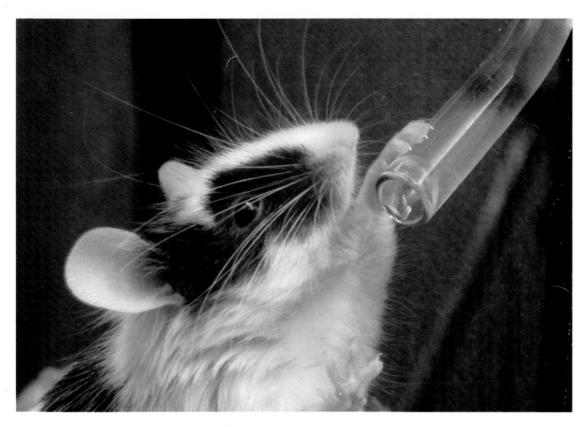

If a mouse gets sick

Like humans, mice sometimes become ill. A sick mouse will usually be listless, and it may try to hide somewhere in the cage. Put it in a spare cage or container immediately. Not all illnesses are contagious, but it's good to play it safe. If you want to do even more to protect the healthy mice, you can clean and disinfect their cage.

There are medications made for small animals, but isolating a mouse and giving it a little extra care is often as effective as treating it with medicine. (It's always best to check with a veterinarian before giving an animal *any* medication.) Place the patient in a warmer-than-usual location, but not over eighty-five degrees F. Give it water, seed, and a bit of its favorite fresh food. Some breeders advise giving a sick mouse something soft to eat such as a small piece of bread soaked in warm milk. Remove uneaten fresh food in ten or fifteen minutes, and wash the dish with soap and water. You can give the mouse more bread in about two hours. Look at the patient often, but don't bother it for several days. Watch your other mice carefully to make sure they are okay. If the sick mouse gets worse or does not improve after two days, you should take it to a veterinarian who takes care of mice.

Remember that prevention is the best treatment for keeping your mice healthy. Be sure to follow these rules:

Keep the cage clean.

Keep the cage in a warm, dry, draft-free area. Don't put it in direct sunlight, and make sure it isn't overheated in summer.

Be sure the cage is properly ventilated; use a wire-mesh cover on glass cages.

Keep all other animals away from the cage.

Avoid overcrowding.

Don't let people with colds near the cage.

Give your mice a balanced diet of seeds, greens, and some additional protein such as good-quality dog biscuits or pelleted food. Don't ever feed them human snack foods!

Remove uneaten fresh food after fifteen minutes.

Wash the waterer, inside and out, with soapy water at least once a week, and replace the water every other day.

Give your mice something hard to chew on.

Keep your mice active; give them toys and an exercise wheel.

Don't add a new mouse to the cage unless it has first been quarantined for seven to ten days.

When a mouse dies

Like all living things, mice eventually die. It's okay to feel sad and cry when a pet dies—you have lost a friend. If you have a yard, you might want to put the body in a small box and bury it. If you don't have a yard, ask your parents to help you think of a good place to bury your pet.

Photographing your mice

If you have a camera, you might enjoy photographing your mice. A camera with a focusing screen is best for this type of photography. Such cameras are known as "SLR" (single lens reflex) cameras. Thirty-five mm SLR cameras usually come with a 50mm lens that can focus on a subject as close as

eighteen inches from the camera. This is adequate for most subjects, but a mouse is so small that it will not show up well if photographed from this distance. You need to get even closer. This can be done by screwing a simple piece of equipment, called a *close-up* lens, onto the front of the camera lens.

Just how close you can get depends on the strength of the close-up lens. These lenses are manufactured in strengths from $+1$ to $+10$. They are usually sold as a set of three lenses, $+1$, $+2$, and $+4$, packed in a small leather case. The lenses can be used individually or screwed together in various combinations, producing a range from $+1$ to $+7$. The sets come in different thread sizes, so it's best to take your camera to the camera store to be fitted.

The glass sides of an aquarium cage can reflect light like a mirror and spoil your photos; the bars of a wooden or wire cage will show and be distracting. The solution is to take the mouse out of the cage and put it on a table near a window. But remember that a mouse moves fast, and it's hard to keep it in focus. Using an electronic flash will help solve this problem. (All the photographs in this book were taken with an electronic flash.) The quick, strong light does not upset mice. Whatever you do, don't take mice outdoors to be photographed.

Photographing small animals is a challenge, but it is also a fascinating hobby. If you keep working at it, you will be happy with the results.

Good luck, and have fun!

Index

About the Author   Jerome Wexler was introduced to photography by his ninth-grade science teacher in an after-school camera club. He has been a professional photographer since 1946 and has had approximately fifteen thousand photographs published all over the world.

Mr. Wexler's photos have always been used for educational purposes. He first worked as an agricultural photographer, taking pictures of all kinds of farming activities as well as good and bad farming practices. The photos were used in advertisements, farm journals, magazines, and textbooks.

What he loves to do most is illustrate—with photographs—children's books on plants, animals, and insects. *Pet Mice* is his thirty-seventh such book. Many have received honors and awards; some have been translated and republished in Japan, China, Germany, Finland, Sweden, Holland, and Great Britain.

Both the Smithsonian Institution and the Agricultural Photo Library, a division of the United States Department of Agriculture, have asked Mr. Wexler to consider leaving them his vast collection of thirty-seven thousand photographs.